My First Book of
CHRISTMAS SONGS

20 Favorite Songs in Easy Piano Arrangements

Bergerac

With Illustrations by
Marty Noble

DOVER PUBLICATIONS, INC.
Mineola, New York

Bibliographical Note

My First Book of Christmas Songs: 20 Favorite Songs in Easy Piano Arrangements is a
new work, first published by Dover Publications, Inc., in 1997.

International Standard Book Number

ISBN-13: 978-0-486-29718-7
ISBN-10: 0-486-29718-7

Manufactured in the United States by Courier Corporation
29718710
www.doverpublications.com

Contents

This one is for Brandon Lewis,
who saw his first Christmas the year this book was written.

". . . it is good to be children sometimes, and never better than at Christmas, when its mighty Founder was a child himself."

Charles Dickens, *A Christmas Carol* (1843)

Christmas songs seem to have been around forever. I remember people singing them when I was a little kid. When I was old enough to learn the words and carry a tune, it was great fun to sing along with everybody else, and to pick out the tunes on our piano with one finger. What a special time of year to wait for!

These days the world seems to spin around faster and faster, and life seems to change quicker and quicker. But those lovely, timeless, sweet and joyous Christmas songs hardly ever change.

Bergerac (Winter 1996)

We Wish You a Merry Christmas

1

O, Come All Ye Faithful

(Adeste Fideles)

English words anonymously
translated from the Latin

Music by J. Reading

Moderate and steady

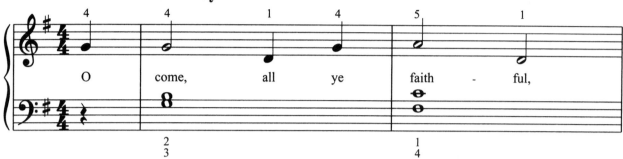

O   come,   all   ye   faith - ful,

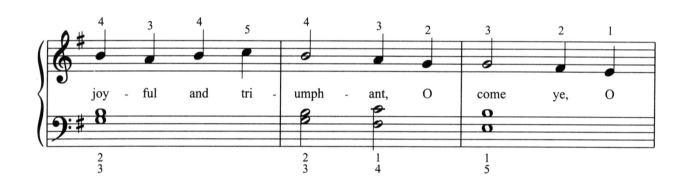

joy - ful   and   tri - umph - ant,   O   come   ye,   O

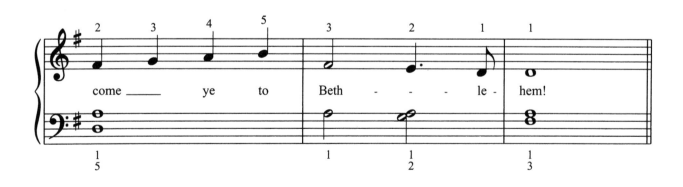

come ____ ye   to   Beth - - - le - hem!

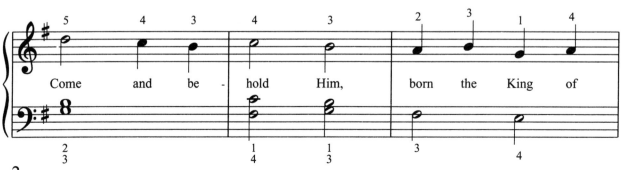

Come   and   be - hold   Him,   born   the   King   of

2

3

Silent Night
(Stille Nacht)

English words anonymously translated
from the German by Joseph Mohr

Music by Franz Gruber (1818)

Tenderly

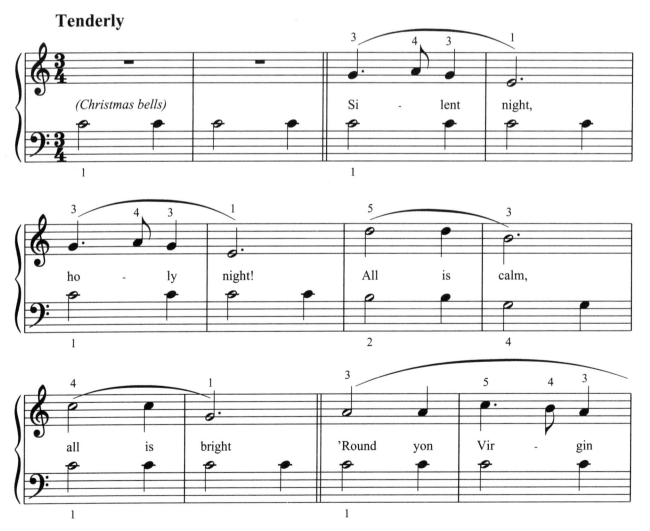

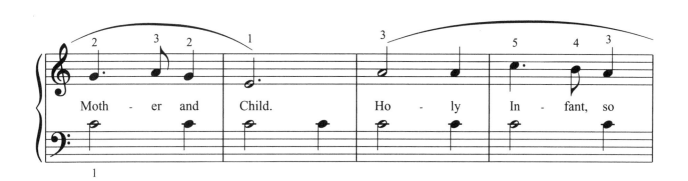

Moth - er and   Child.   Ho - ly   In - fant, so

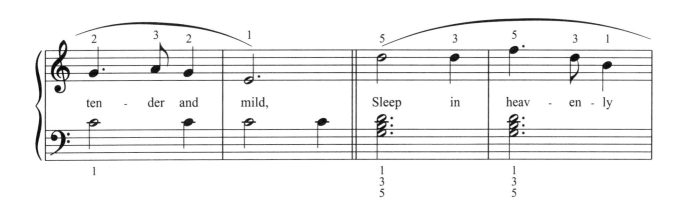

ten - der and   mild,   Sleep   in   heav - en - ly

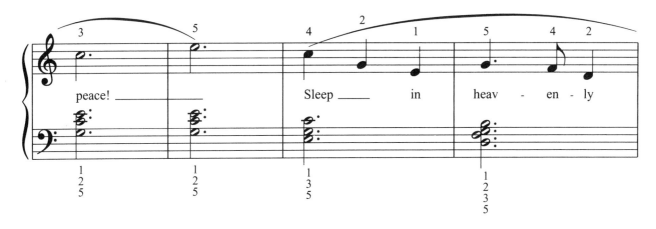

peace! ____   ____   Sleep ____   in   heav - en - ly

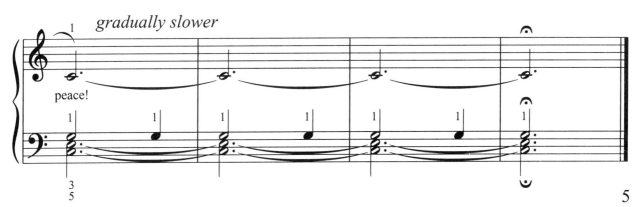

gradually slower

peace!

5

Joy to the World

Words by Isaac Watts (1719)

Composer unknown

Spirited and strong

Joy to the world! The Lord is come! Let earth re - ceive her

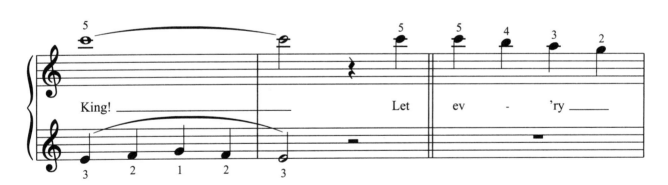

King! _____ Let ev - 'ry _____

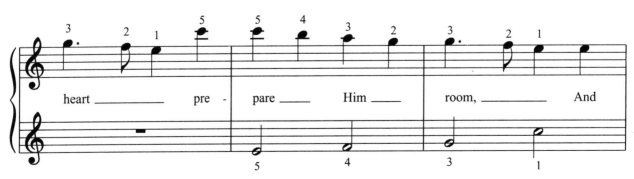

heart _____ pre - pare _____ Him _____ room, _____ And

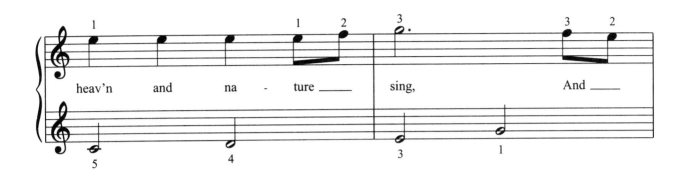

heav'n and na - ture _____ sing, And _____

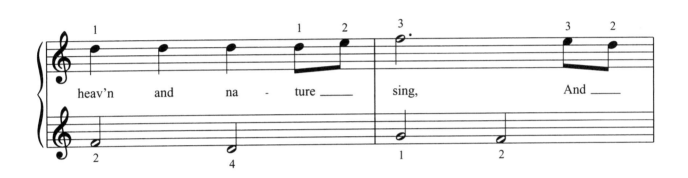

heav'n and na - ture _____ sing, And _____

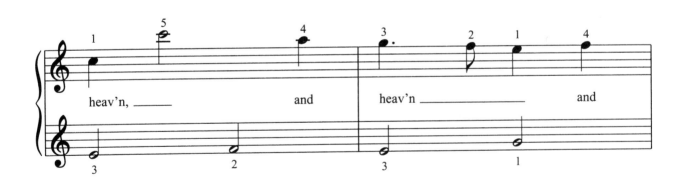

heav'n, _____ and heav'n _____ and

na - ture sing! _____

What Child Is This?

Words by William C. Dix (19th c.)

Music: "Greensleeves"
(English folk song)

Sadly, but moving ahead

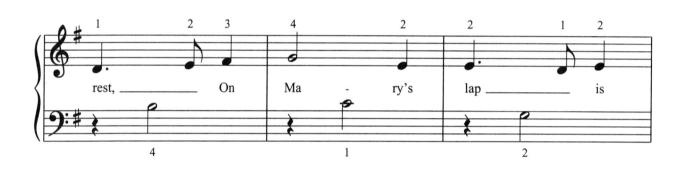

What Child is this, _____ who, laid to

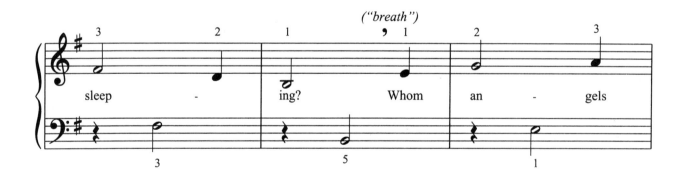

rest, _____ On Ma - ry's lap _____ is

("breath")

sleep - ing? Whom an - gels

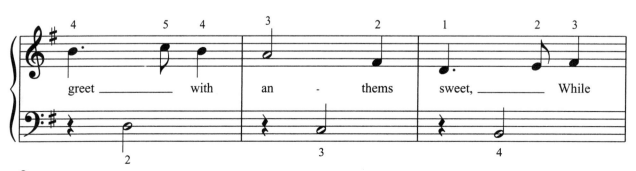

greet _____ with an - thems sweet, _____ While

8

Brighter

gradually slower and quieter

9

Hark! The Herald Angels Sing

Words by Charles Wesley (18th c.)

Music by Felix Mendelssohn

Bright and sprightly

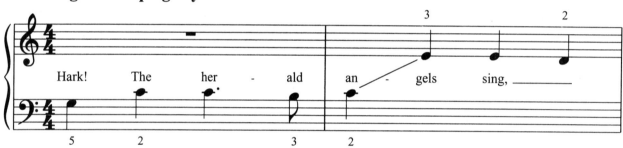

Hark! The her - ald an - gels sing,

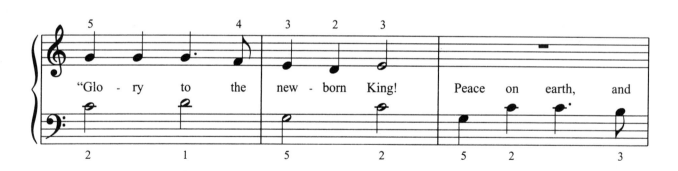

"Glo - ry to the new - born King! Peace on earth, and

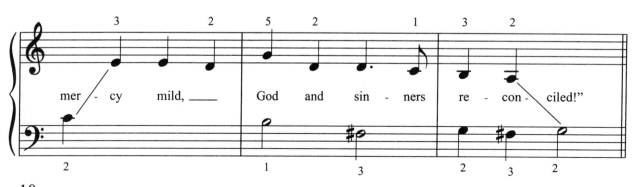

mer - cy mild, ___ God and sin - ners re - con - ciled!"

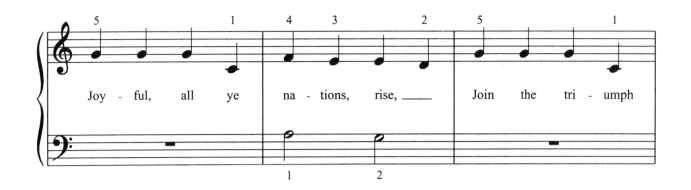

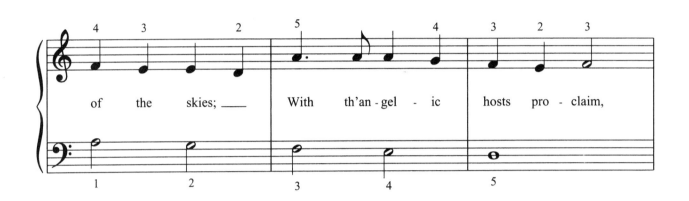

The First Nowell

Traditional Christmas song,
possibly French

With good spirit, not too slow

The ____ first _____ No - well the ____

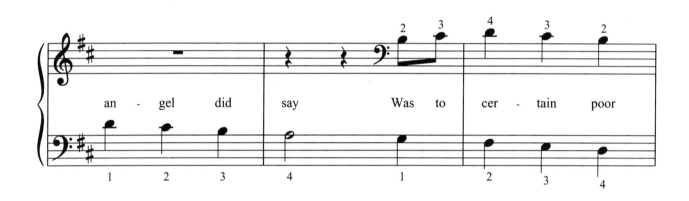

an - gel did say Was to cer - tain poor

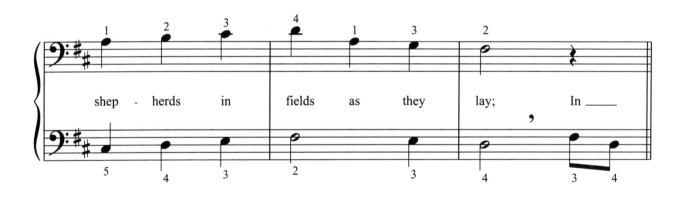

shep - herds in fields as they lay; In ____

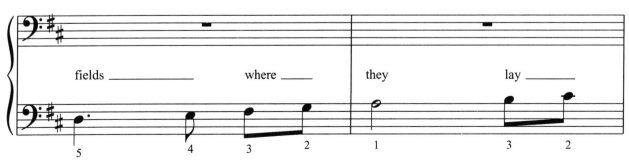

fields _____ where ____ they lay _____

12

O Come, O Come, Emmanuel

English words translated from the Latin
by John Mason Neale (19th c.)

Church chant

Gently flowing

O come, O come, Em - man - - u -

el, And ran - som cap - tive Is - - ra -

el, That mourns in lone - ly ex - - ile

14

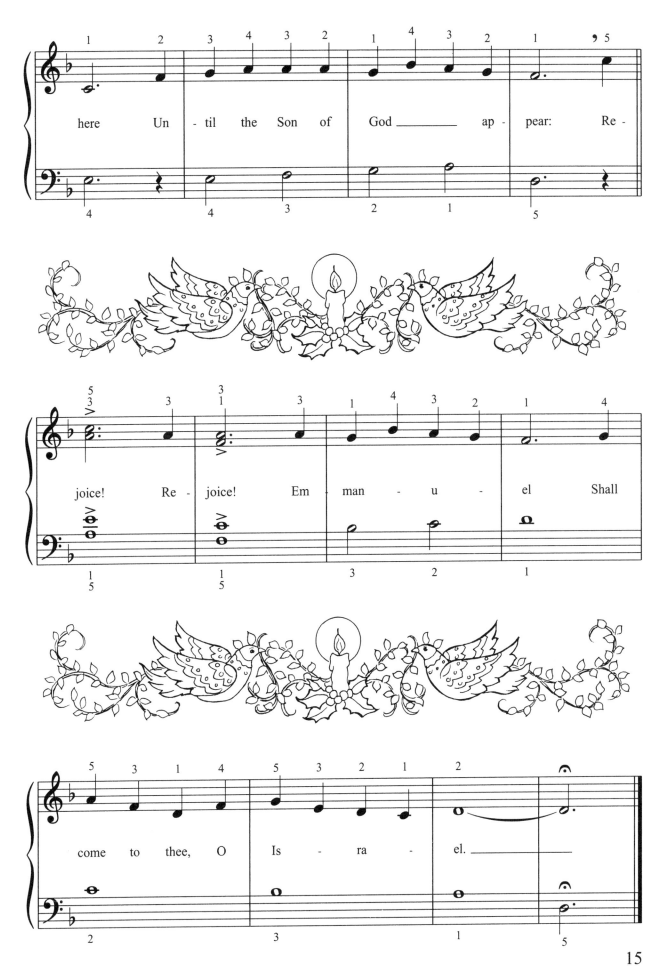

here Un - til the Son of God _____ ap - pear: Re -

joice! Re - joice! Em - man - u - el Shall

come to thee, O Is - ra - el. _____

O Christmas Tree

(O Tannenbaum)

Traditional English words

Traditional German

Very subdued and peaceful

O Christ - mas tree, O Christ - mas tree, How

stead - fast are your bran - ches! Your

boughs are green in sum - mer's clime And

through the snows of win - ter - time. O Christ - mas tree, O

Christ - mas tree, How stead - fast are your bran - ches!

16

Jingle Bells

(One-Horse Open Sleigh)

Words and music by James Pierpont (1859)

Bright, light

18

Deck the Hall

Words and music by Thomas Oliphant (19th c.)

Quickly, with a lot of spirit

Deck the hall with boughs of hol - ly,

Fa la la la la, la la la la! 'Tis the sea - son

to be jol - ly, Fa la la la la, la la la la!

Pat-a-pan

Original French words by Bernard de la Monnaye

Traditional Burgundian
dance-song (ca. 1700)

Always moving forward, like a march

[Beat your drum! Sound your fife!
And while you're playing
Ture lurelu pata pat-a-pan
We shall gaily sing about Noël!]

The Coventry Carol

(Lully, lullay)

Words by Robert Croo (1534)

Traditional English

Plaintively, but not too slow

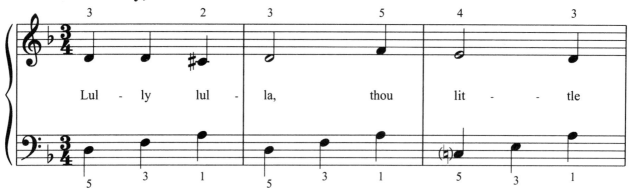

Lul - ly lul - la, thou lit - tle

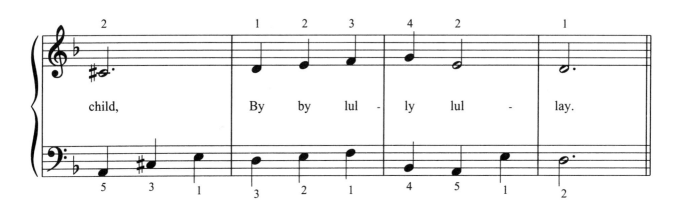

child, By by lul - ly lul - lay.

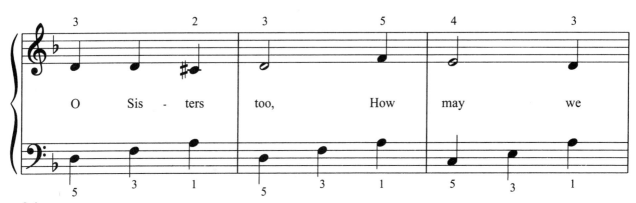

O Sis - ters too, How may we

24

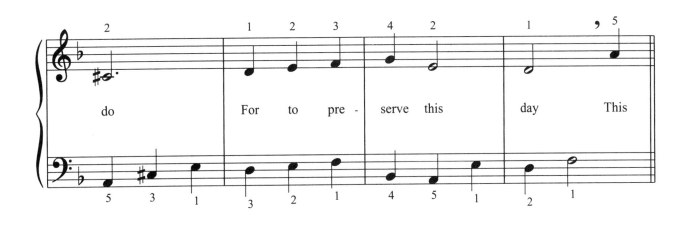

do   For to pre - serve this   day   This

poor   young - ling   For   whom   we   do

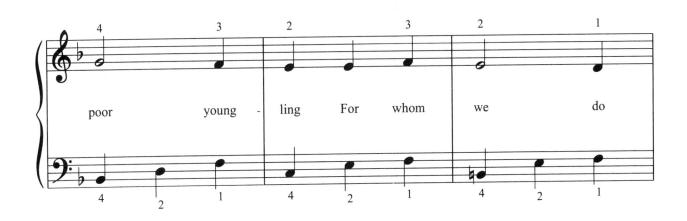

sing   By   by lul - ly lul - lay?

God Rest Ye Merry, Gentlemen

Traditional English

Slow, peaceful, unhurried

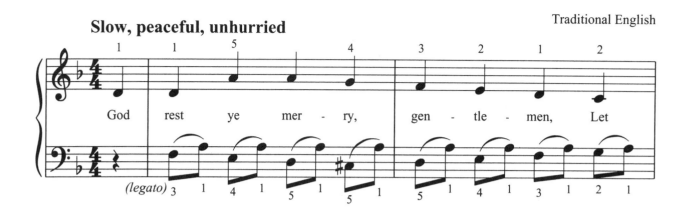

God rest ye mer - ry, gen - tle - men, Let

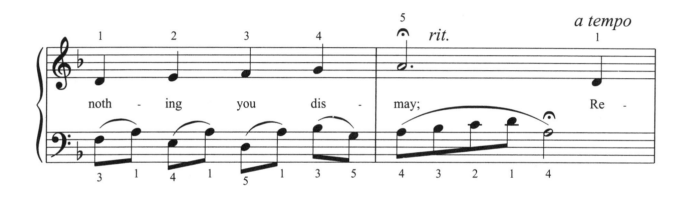

noth - ing you dis - may; Re -

mem - ber Christ, our Sa - viour, Was

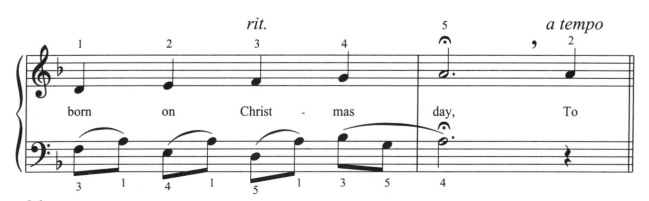

born on Christ - mas day, To

(the left hand always legato and unhurried)

Away in a Manger

Anonymous words

Music by James R. Murray ? (ca. 1887)

29

The Song of the Birds

(Al veure despuntar)

Traditional Catalan carol

Flowing and expressive

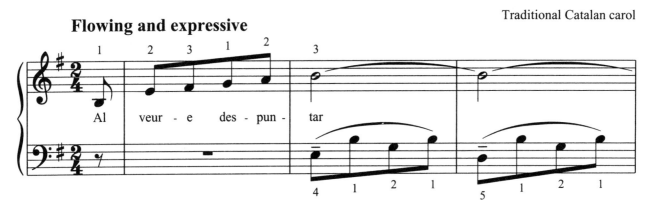

Al veur - e des - pun - tar

lo ma - jor llu - mi - nar

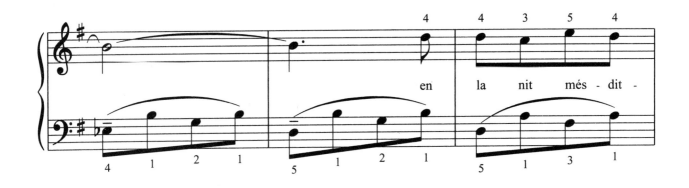

en la nit més - dit -

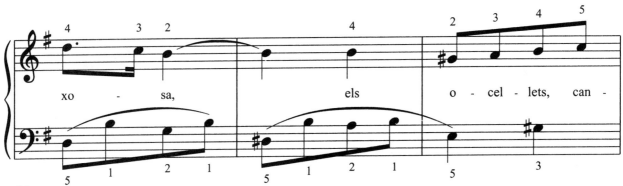

xo - sa, els o - cel - lets, can -

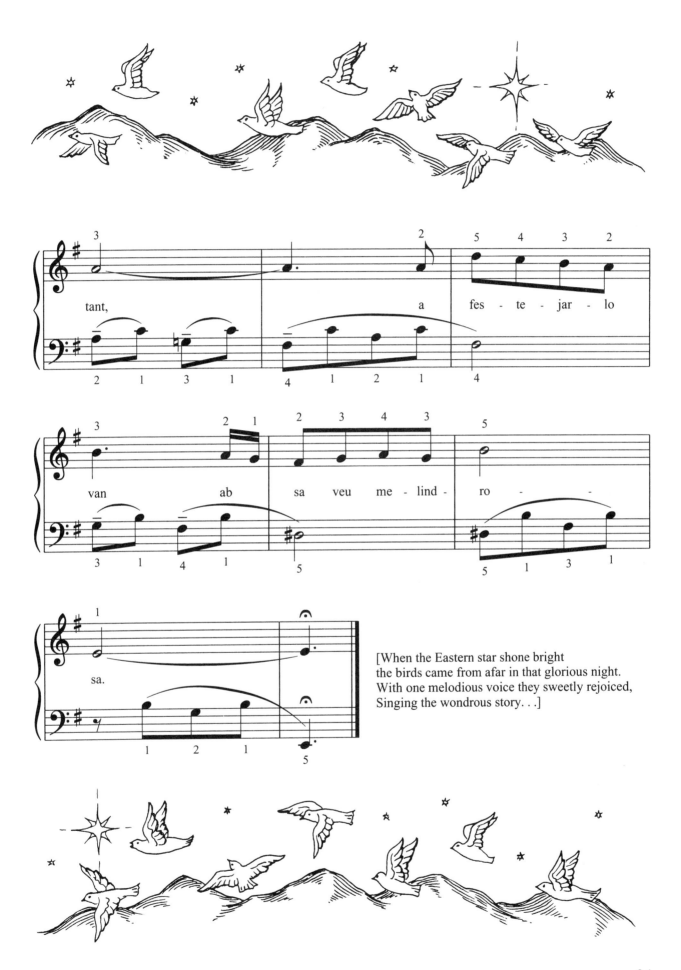

[When the Eastern star shone bright
the birds came from afar in that glorious night.
With one melodious voice they sweetly rejoiced,
Singing the wondrous story. . .]

We Three Kings of Orient Are

Words and Music by John H. Hopkins, Jr. (ca. 1857)

A moderately slow processional

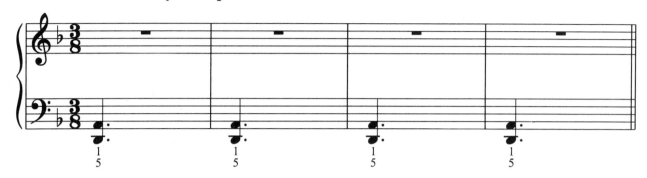

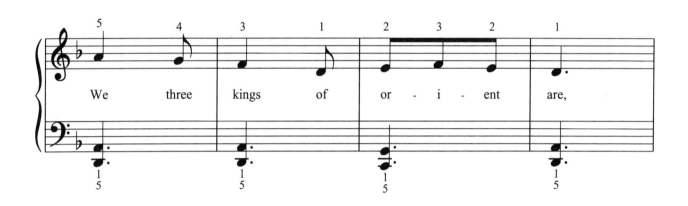

We three kings of or - i - ent are,

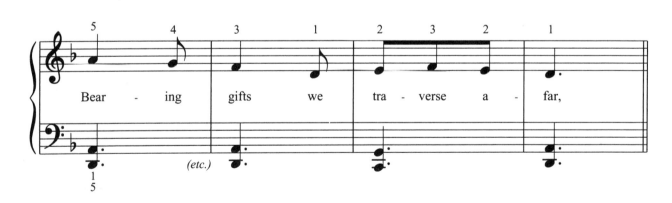

Bear - ing gifts we tra - verse a - far,

(etc.)

Field and foun - tain, moor and moun - tain,

(etc.)

32

Angels We Have Heard on High

(Cantique de Noël)

Traditional English words

Traditional French carol

Lively, with a good beat

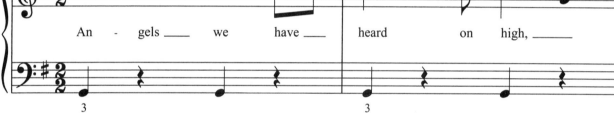

An - gels ___ we have ___ heard on high, ___

Sweet - ly ___ sing - ing ___ o'er the plains, And the ___ moun - tain ___

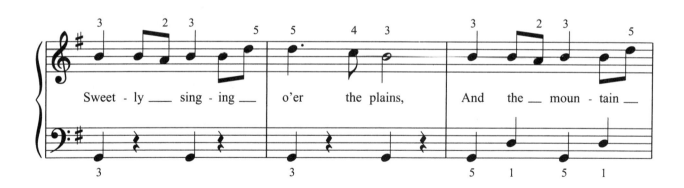

in re - ply, ___ Ech - o - ing their ___ joy - ous strains.

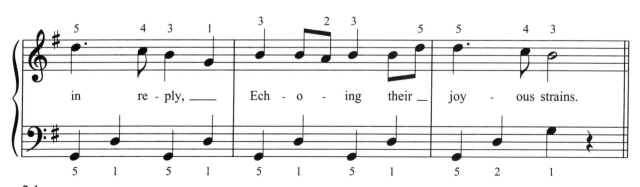

Glo - - - - - - - -

o - - - o - ri - a!

in ex - cel - sis De - o, De - o.

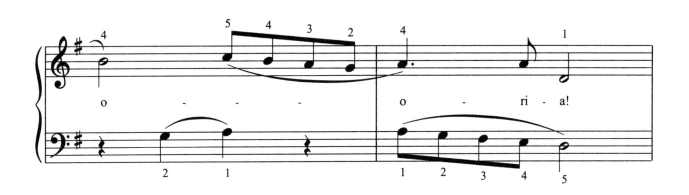

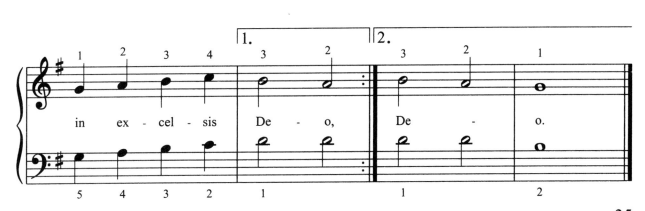

O Little Town of Bethlehem

Words by Phillips Brooks (19th c.)   Music by Lewis H. Redner (19th c.)

Gently, quietly

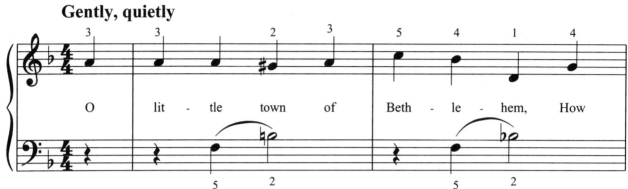

O lit - tle town of Beth - le - hem, How

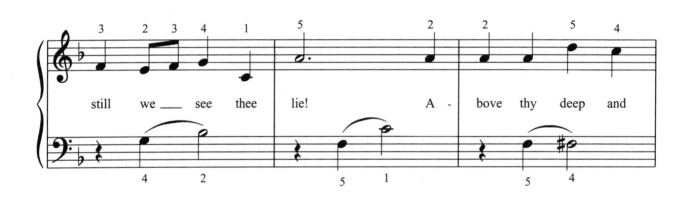

still we ___ see thee lie! A - bove thy deep and

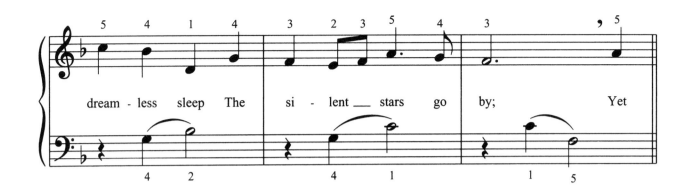

dream - less sleep The si - lent ___ stars go by; Yet

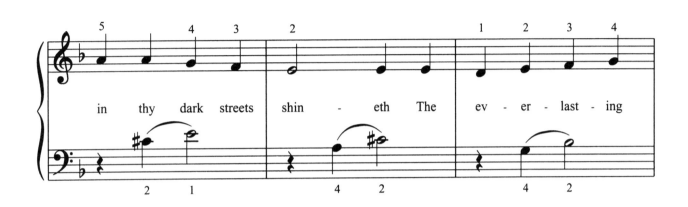

in thy dark streets shin - eth The ev - er - last - ing

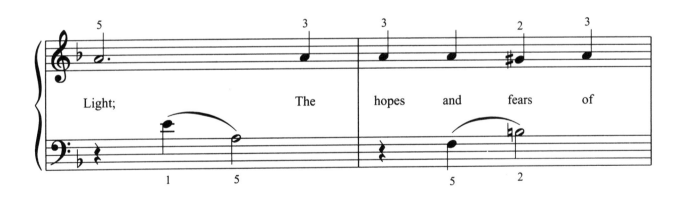

Light; The hopes and fears of

slower 'till the end

all the years Are met in thee to - night.

Shepherds, O Shepherds!

(Pasztorek, Pasztorek)

Start slowly, then faster at each repetition

Traditional Hungarian dance-song

[Shepherds, O shepherds!
Come rejoice this night
of wonder and joy!]

Repeat as often as you like,
each time faster than before.

**The Pieces Arranged
in Their Approximate Order of Difficulty**
(from easy to beginning-intermediate)